Choice.

Please.

WRITTEN BY: DR. KIM

Table of Contents:

I.   Freedom of Choice?

II.   Informed Consent

III.   2008

IV.   2009

V.   2011

VI.   2015

VII.   2016

VIII. Perspective

FREEDOM OF CHOICE?

Wouldn't it make sense that in the United States, the land of the free and the home of the brave, we would have the freedom of choice? Sure. It's a concept that many think we do have. However, the more I research and open my eyes to DAILY happenings around me in the world of politics, the media and other strategies, I am beginning to disagree.

Advertising strategies, peer pressure and popularities in society can cause us to hesitate when faced with a choice; sometimes an EXTREMELY important choice. For example, an apple at the grocery store would most likely be cheaper if it were not in the organic section. Even something as simple as choosing the right apple for your family may be difficult, knowing the benefits of eating organic combined with the weekly grocery budget.

If you see or hear something repetitively enough, it will stick in your brain. If you are unaware that there are actually people that go against the crowd, against popular belief, it could quite possibly be assumed that there is only one way to go. If you are shown that a particular thing is wonderful, fabulous and only positive, that will be the picture painted in your head. Various television commercials are advertising options that are, in my opinion, the opposite of natural remedies to stay healthy. Sometimes images of happy people living life are used to portray the benefits of the item being advertised, yet if you were to close your eyes and listen intently to the words of the commercial, the picture painted would most likely be different...especially the parts of the commercial that mention side effects of such unnatural things. If they showed images of people who were suffering those side effects, perhaps it would not SEEM like such a popular choice.

Currently in 2016, so many places offer vaccines that most people see or hear numerous times that they are available. Just driving down the street in even a small town will typically present opportunities for you to conveniently go get them. If you see advertising daily, you may assume that's just what people do.

Well, I'm here to tell you, that I have learned a lot about myself so far in this life and it's safe to say that I am not one that just runs with the crowd. I think for myself. I research. I choose natural methods first, every time. I pay attention to the ingredients and the side effects of various things, from what my family eats to what options we choose in order to maintain good health.

I have noticed that most mothers are unaware that they have MANY choices to make regarding what happens to their baby – or not – right after birth, especially when birth occurs in a hospital. If people are unaware that choices even exist, is that still freedom of choice?

Some first-time mothers are even unaware that there are MANY options for where to have a child: in the woods, in a car, at home, etc. It is important to note that a hospital birth is not required to birth a child. In explaining why some mothers choose a hospital, fear of the unknown is often the answer given.

If a hospital is the method by which the mother chooses to have the baby, even more choices exist during labor and when the baby is born. Will the mother choose an epidural? Will the mother choose to have the baby circumcised? Will the mother choose to have antibiotic eye drops?

INFORMED CONSENT

Somethings just piss me off, no matter how hard I try to not let them. For instance, if all mothers who presented at the pediatrician for their child's scheduled MMR (measles, mumps, rubella) vaccine were given a piece of paper to inform them that ABORTED FETAL TISSUE was still present as a WI-38 human diploid fibroblast cell [1], would they then still make the choice they presumably were going to make? That is just one ingredient of one example of how our so called freedom of choice confuses me. If the COMPLETE list of ingredients (THIMEROSAL ANYONE?) were given, perhaps even more mothers would think about options.

When people go in for their yearly flu shot, many are unaware that some still also contain aborted fetal material, coded differently as PER C6[1]. I guess if you're given a list of ingredients and you haven't gone to medical school, (which is most of the world) simply calling it ABORTED BABY is WAY too much to stomach. So if they call it *blah blah blah*, it will not have such an impeccable impact, as would giving people the description of the code.

That's the thing about abortion. It's a choice for a woman to make. For me, being as blunt as I can be, I would not choose that for myself. Once that fetus has a heartbeat, which is usually between day ten and day twenty, it is alive – in my opinion. When that heartbeat stops, whether a car accident or abortion, life is then ended. To me, abortion is not a positive thing.

I do know that good exists and that evil also exists. Way before I was alive, a mother decided to end her child's life. The tissue from that aborted child's body was then used as an experiment – a HUGE one - cells from it were used to concoct a vaccine, which is now commonly injected into the children of the Earth. Gross. Abortion, in my opinion, is evil. People want to take that evil, put it in a mixture and make me inject it into my child SIMPLY in order for them to attend public school? Uh, what?

Last year, in 2015, the state of California voted to mandate all scheduled vaccines to attend public school. Not only does it mandate those currently listed on schedule, but any future vaccine schedule changes deemed necessary. Oh my! If that alone doesn't make you confused, it should.

My friends that currently live in California were OUTRAGED. Freedom of choice, anyone? I lived in California for less than a year and fell head over heels in love with the ocean & the atmosphere. It's difficult for me to not feel a strong connection to what's happening there. When this law, SB277 was approved, my first thought was THANK GOD I currently live in Nebraska where I still have a religious exemption to vaccination available so my kid can merely go to school.

I guess you could say I have a SUPER STRONG belief system. One of my girlfriends used to tell me that its quite apparent *I like what I like*. That holds true for most things in my life. Growing up we chose natural methods first, ALWAYS.

My education surrounding this topic began in Catholic High School. I learned about abortion, and how the church completely disagrees – I thought. I was taught that it was EVIL. I was taught that it was wrong. I was taught that it was a sin – no matter what. I was taught that a fetus is the same as a baby which is the same as a life. I began to develop a strong feeling of dislike for anything surrounding abortion. So, in order to attend Catholic high school, my parents signed a religious exemption to vaccination form. THAT'S RIGHT... I wasn't fully vaccinated and I'm still alive. Can you believe it? It's like I'm coming out of the closet or something to say that so publicly.

Another important lesson I learned in high school was that our bodies are a gift and are to be cherished. They are temples. It was frowned upon to take any action against holding our bodies in that high regard.

After high school, my Jesuit University was very medically focused, and given my want to be a natural healer I often felt like an outsider. Since I had not been fully vaccinated, to enter that University, I simply had to sign a waiver that forced me to leave campus if an outbreak of something I could have been vaccinated for appeared. Well you better believe I voluntarily would leave campus. You bet. No problem. I took many science classes, including genetics and evolution. I was kind of a nerd.

After college graduation I then attended chiropractic school, with my doctorate degree giving me full knowledge of how the body works, with its innate healing potential. It was amazing to me how beautifully we were designed as living creatures. For the creator above to give us defense mechanisms to fight disease, as simple as nose hairs, good bacteria and an IMMUNE SYSTEM, it was quite obvious to me that we were born to get sick, to fight disease and to win.

There are a few (maybe many) things in this world that make me heated, at least a little. You could say I'm passionate. I have always been in awe of those throughout history that have stood up for freedom, yet I didn't feel the need to even tell the world my strong opinion until my blood pressure rose significantly. I was just fine in my little world living how I wanted.

That was until SB277. I related so much with the people in California that I became physically unable to be silent. I started to speak out about abortion, about vaccines, about mandated medical procedures and genetic reactions to certain ingredients. Just when I thought that simply stating my choice to not vaccinate my children was enough for me to be calmer, I was given more news.

The Catholic diocese in my area decided that the current vaccine schedule was now required to attend school, except for those with aborted fetal tissue. Literally the minute I learned about this, I started making phone calls. I called fellow doctors. ALL of the doctors I called felt the same way I did, however, for various reasons they felt as though their hands were tied. They would rather not speak out. I called my high school priest, who is still in the same archdiocese and he was COMPLETELY unaware that aborted fetal material ever existed in vaccinations. I called the attorney for the archdiocese. He basically told me that I should be glad they aren't forcing me to inject my kids with the complete schedule, including the vaccines containing aborted fetal material.

You see, aborted fetal material injected into my kids is one thing, animal genetics is another. If our bodies should be respected as temples, which I believe they should be, I also cannot wrap my brain around the genes from another species being injected into my kids. The purpose of that foreign code is to react with our human genes. That's also gross to me.

A religious exemption is intended to allow us to hold strong and true to our belief system, whatever that is, for whatever reason that is. You could say that the news of this made my blood pressure rise again, instantly. I am not a fan of force. No thank you. I am not a fan of control. No thank you. I am not a fan of forced medical procedures, especially when they are present to simply allow my child to attend the same school I attended, using the same paperwork that I used to attend. Uh, no thank you.

After the knowledge of that change, I daily became even more unable to be silent. I began to call State Senators, U.S. Senators, Governors and other influential people in the world that could potentially make a difference.

Now I know that life is not fair, but I also know that sins of omission are as real as sins of action. I felt completely unable to not take action given EVERY possible opportunity. Even in movies, like the most recent James Bond film, when vaccines are mentioned, my husband will give me a look of *oh my, please don't freak out.* It is extremely hard to bite my tongue.

For some reason, as time goes on, I feel more and more comfortable speaking in a room full of people about my opinions, no matter who those people are. Whether about abortion, vaccination, or health in general, if it affects my world and potentially my children, I can feel what seems like my heart beating literally out of my chest so intensely that I am physically unable to stay quiet.

Not only is aborted fetal material currently used in multiple vaccines today, it is also used throughout the country in medical research. A lot. From large scale research companies to small town community college nursing school projects, students are commonly required to complete multiple lab experiments using REAL aborted fetal material. Again, gross.

These things are not discussed as often as I think they should be. Some people haven't become aware of these issues, some people are too fearful to speak out and some don't care. Well I am aware and I do care. I find that my significant heartbeat in certain situations trumps any fear that could sneak in.

Each person on this planet is different, with different opinions, that make people choose various options. My journey of motherhood thus far has been filled with many decisions about health and about life in general.

2008

There I was, taking thirty-five hours of classes and labs in my last year of professional school, seeing numerous patients in the student clinic, working two part-time jobs as a receptionist at a chiropractic office and at a fabulous hair salon, studying for board exams, helping as a teacher's assistant and......my period was late.

I had a VERY unsettling feeling in my soul that my monthly friend did not want to visit anytime soon. Some say - when you know you know - and even though I didn't want to know or couldn't even wrap my brain around the idea of being pregnant, my intuition and my soul YELLED otherwise.

In between classes on a sunny and cold January day I found myself with enough courage to step foot into what now seems super ironic - Planned Parenthood - for a complimentary pregnancy test.

It was an experience SO FAR out of my comfort zone that recalling it now was almost an out of body experience. The whole entire pregnancy seemed to put me in such a state of shock and fear that I was unable to live comfortably in my own skin. I had been a confident person, at least I thought so, until this point in my life.

They say not to tell yourself that it won't happen to you, but I guess I did. The memories I have are mostly from a perspective of someone else, watching myself do these things.

I do remember peeing in a cup while feeling like a fearful high school girl. I wasn't in my teens though, I was twenty-six and almost a doctor. After I turned in the cup, I took a seat in the lobby of Planned Parenthood, surrounded by other women. I scanned the crowd, trying to feel comfortable. That's the thing though, how in the world does anyone begin to feel comfortable at a time like this? It was uncharted territory. I could possibly be pregnant. It hit me like nothing ever before. I didn't even know how to begin to feel about that possibility.

Now I know that it takes two to tango and I wasn't the Virgin Mary, but I never really believed unplanned pregnancy was in my future. So here is a HUGE shout out to all those who also feel it won't happen to you, it sure can!

The mere minutes it took for the nurse to say my name to get me out of that waiting room seemed to move slower than ANY OTHER time prior. I was frozen. I couldn't focus to even read a magazine. I was in between classes and had a

CPR final later that day so I tried to focus on what to remember for the exam.

After what seemed to be a decade of time, a short unhappy looking lady finally called my name. I went into a room without a patient bed and knew from the surroundings and the look on her face that I was indeed pregnant.

I sat down. The nurse pulled out some materials. I was almost shaking at the mere thought of what options were in that paperwork. I was at Planned Parenthood of all places. If I wanted options, this was the place to be.

The nurse seemed to have very little time for me. She told me quickly that I was pregnant and asked multiple times if I wanted to hear my options. I was SPEECHLESS. I knew in my soul that even HEARING the word ABORTION gave me the creeps so that option was out.

The fourth time she asked, I'm sure my strong tone indicated that I was not a fan of abortion and that I needed time to process the news. I took the information from her and asked her for a minute alone to think about things. The information included options for abortion, adoption and what to expect during pregnancy. My hands shook when throwing them down on the desk.

I literally could not stand to try to exit the room. I called my mom who was nothing short of ecstatic to hear the news. She had always wanted to be a grandmother. I was unable to handle any excitement. I told her that I didn't know how to feel. I was so surprised, in shock and almost crabby about it. I was about to finish my doctorate degree and heal the world. This was not in my plans.

Looking back now, I realize that plans do not belong to us as humans. We were put on this earth with purpose and our plan only comes to life if it aligns with our purpose. However, the thought of someone saying THAT to me in that moment would have probably only made me crabbier.

I told my mom that I loved her and hung up the phone. I mustered up enough confidence to leave Planned Parenthood and went to my CPR final.

Pregnant in School

School was a fantastic distraction for my brain to have plenty of time to get used to the idea of being a mother. Now please don't get me wrong - I always knew I had the want to be a mother - my mother was fabulous – I just wasn't quite prepared mentally for it to be so soon, especially since I had only ONE year before graduation. Not too long after I found out that I rocked my CPR final, I started to have morning sickness.

Morning sickness is the STUPIDEST name for it - it lasted all day. In the middle of morning class – BAM – the smell of the cafeteria – BAM – the thought of the cadaver lab – BAM – when in the quiet library – BAM – at work – BAM. Whenever it wanted, morning sickness took over.

That next Saturday morning, I was supposed to open up at work and I couldn't stop vomiting. I called in sick, which I had NEVER done before, and told them the news. Saying it out loud sounded so foreign to my ears. I knew the only way to get more comfortable with the news, was to say it out loud more often.

I felt so ill and was so exhausted that I continued to not enjoy being in my own skin. That was an odd feeling. In high school I loved being me. I was involved in almost everything – dance team, cheerleading, one act, drama, speech, volleyball, and more. I was prom queen and then ended up getting a half scholarship to Creighton University before professional school. I had kept my journey thus far on track with my want to be a doctor. Now how was I going to do it all while being pregnant?

Each morning would feel uncomfortable and different. Almost like a dream. I slowly began to tell my friends the news. It's amazing how quickly you find out who your true friends are in times of change. Some were happy for me. Some stopped coming around since I was sick, tired and didn't want to do anything fun.

Anyone who knew me, knew that I was the most positive energetic person prior to the news. Life was a joy. The thought of motherhood for most is also a joy, but for me, as a surprise unplanned pregnancy, the joy was difficult to find. I was usually mentally strong. I knew what I liked, I knew words were just words and I knew my own opinion of myself was the ONLY thing that mattered.

I continued to go to class, work as a receptionist part-time, see patients in the clinic, work as a teacher's assistant and study for boards, if any energy was left over, which was usually not much at all. Soon my wardrobe was too small, like it happened overnight. It's quite intense how something as understandably simple as needing bigger clothes due to pregnancy can hit your confidence level like a semi-truck. I began to feel even more uncomfortable in my own skin. In college I had tried to stay fit with exercise. Health is a thing I strive for daily. Although I knew that I was pregnant and larger clothes were inevitable, I no longer felt fit.

A few months later, the hormones were beginning to regulate, the sickness and fatigue were getting less and less, and then I went for a routine ultrasound. The ultrasound tech had another unseen look on her face. More news: twins. Change was and is inevitable, and I thought I could handle anything but this was difficult. I think overwhelm is the biggest feeling that hit me. I was already juggling so much and now I was given a larger challenge.

Soon after, I began to feel the twins move inside my womb. Each kick softened my heart. I was now able to focus on the love growing for them. It made the situation more real and soon I started to FINALLY feel a connection to them. I was beginning to feel a want to be a mother NOW - not just someday. Prior to that, it was just shock.

I began to imagine how cute they would look in the little outfits I would see. I had a love unknown for little beings I'd never met. Each day I would feel a stronger connection to them.

I kept going to my classes, rocking the exams, sleeping a lot, working as much as possible and I tried to save a little energy to still have a social life. I got asked to sing in a friend's wedding in May that year and for the first time I was beginning to feel confident enough to sing again in public. Singing for me has always taken great courage and confidence, even when I was not pregnant.

The Wedding

I was so excited to sing and feel confident doing it, while pregnant. I was beginning to enjoy being me again. At the wedding, I sang my heart out and loved every minute of it. Immediately after the wedding, I felt the need to run to the bathroom. I'll spare the details, but I knew that something unexpected was again about to happen, given what occurred in the bathroom of that church. I had a heavy sinking in my tummy that this pregnancy may not make it full-term. That night my water broke at only five months along.

I was told that unless I can make it a minimum of two more weeks, the babies would be too young to take to the NICU. So I tried to become mentally prepared to stay in that hospital, stuck in that bed for at least two weeks. I was fearful, alone even in the presence of others, terrified and confused. I was uncomfortable at its extreme, in my own body. Instead of two weeks, I made it two days. Then the pain started. It was more intense than anything imaginable. That's probably why people have a hard time relating to labor pains unless they've experienced them. There's NOTHING in the world that's even remotely comparable.

Labor was starting. Here they come. The doctor kept saying - now you know there's nothing we can do, because they are too early for the NICU. *Shut up lady* is the feeling I had and didn't voice. Instead, I responded with, yes, I understand. I was emotionless, frozen and in shock.

The babies were born separately. The first came out breathing, with a heartbeat and she tried to open her eyes. I held her for about a half hour, waiting for her heart to stop and then she assumingly went to heaven. She was too premature for the NICU so I just held her until she stopped breathing. I remember saying to her - Go back to Heaven, I love you. Those were the only words I could find. Looking back now, I have no idea how I was able to say that. I was in such shock that I didn't know how to feel or what to say or what to do. The second baby's contractions began immediately after the first went to heaven. Almost like she wanted to be with her sister. The second baby was smaller and didn't try to open her eyes. When she was born, her heart was beating and she was breathing, also for about a half hour. She was then sent back to heaven. There was not a single thing I could do to change or control what had happened. I had no choice.

That hour was the fastest block of time I have ever, EVER experienced. I don't remember much from that night in the hospital. This is where time sped up. I remember white sheets, bad smells, a helpless feeling, confusion and disbelief as days went on.

When I was about to be released from the hospital, various people came into the room for various reasons. A professional complimentary photographer offered to take pictures of the twins. I struggled with saying yes. They were still laying in the bassinet, lifeless and cold. I agreed, but I was unaware of what I was really agreeing to.

They began to take pictures, and then they wanted me to hold them again. It was so odd to hold their lifeless bodies. After the photo shoot, someone came in to take them out of the room for transportation to a funeral home. The memory of them being wheeled out of the room is vivid in my mind. I couldn't stop them, even if I wanted to. I had no choice. I wanted that moment to stand still. That was the last minute I physically shared a room with those babies.

I was shaking when I went to the funeral home to have them cremated. Immediately I was struck with a feeling that wow, life is temporary. BOOM. To fully and significantly wrap my conscious brain around that so blown-up-in-my-face idea was now as easy as saying duh.

Some say that until you have an experience that throws that fact – that life is temporary – in your face, you cannot fully comprehend exactly what it means. Anyone who has ever lost a child, a sibling, a parent, etc., can most likely relate. It may seem negative, but every human dies. Every single human. We could go at any time because tomorrow is not guaranteed.

Walking across the street can be as dangerous and getting struck by lightning. I've learned that in order to slightly be okay with that concept, as much as I possibly can be, I have to learn ways to better appreciate each moment, since the current moment is the only one we really have.

It took a while for me to even be a little bit accepting of what had happened. I remember waking up the first morning back in my apartment, sitting up so quickly, hoping for the nightmare I vividly remembered to all be a dream. At least that was EXACTLY how it felt. I didn't want it to be real. It was.

Temporary Routine

Just as life is temporary, so was my typical student routine. I was twenty-six years old and had been a student since age four. My usual day for my whole existence up to this point in time was education, learning and for sure some fun moments. It felt impossible to jump into the fun moments when all I felt inside my soul was confusion, sadness and a shocked feeling of the events of the past year.

I then received notice that my temporary routine was going to be changed sooner than I anticipated. I had passed all classes, fulfilled my clinic requirements early and I was eligible for a preceptorship before graduation - anywhere I wanted to go. I had met student chiropractors from all over the world with fascinating perspectives. I had flown to California previously to interview at more than two handfuls of offices from Ventura county down the coast to Carlsbad, near San Diego. I found a few I liked, with my favorite in Thousand Oaks, California.

I was planning on moving in October and all of this change kept me well distracted. That's a crazy thing - distraction. Whether we do it to ourselves consciously, or media sources keep our subconscious and conscious brains occupied, our mind is capable of powerful mechanisms to allow us to cope – well most of us at least.

As time went on, no matter how hard I tried to ignore the pain, the coping mechanisms of grief inevitably hit me, quite often. Anytime I would see a double stroller made for twins, I would get upset. Sad moments in movies stimulated tears much easier. I was anemic, dehydrated, almost finished with my doctorate degree and very short-fused.

They say that anger is a good part of the healing process of grief, but I still struggled with the sense of being completely comfortable in my own body. I was extremely hard on myself for how I looked in the mirror. Those that knew me then weren't typically included in "my moments" of grief. I hung out alone by choice and slept a lot.

California

It was only a couple months later that I was on a jet with six giant suitcases to Los Angeles, California with a one-way ticket. I have visited California a few times before and absolutely fell in love with the atmosphere. Growing up in small town Nebraska, I appreciated California's openness for different cultures, its breathtaking views, and opportunities to defeat my quick boredom. I continued to stay busy.

I found peace big time at the beach, from the movement of the ocean. I remember sitting in the sand in Malibu, watching the waves and feeling my heart instantly slow down. There were so many things to do and to see, I rarely was even aware that I was grieving. That's the thing I've learned about grief - if you don't allow yourself to fully live in the moment, life will pass you by and all of a sudden a mental trigger will stop you in your tracks.

I quickly found an apartment with a short beautiful commute through the mountains to my preceptorship in Thousand Oaks. After only a few days, I learned of a nearby country club that was hiring a bartender. I got the job and was instantly even busier.

Grief can easily be triggered by daily situations and circumstances. I'll never forget when the first trigger hit me. I was on break at an evening shift at the country club when I checked my phone and learned that a friend from chiropractic school had just given birth to a stillborn baby. Had I made it full-term with the twins, they would have been born at the same time. It hit me so hard that it was almost as if I was reliving my experience in present day. I hadn't taken much time at this point in my life to heal. I couldn't. I wasn't ready. I didn't know how. I know that now. I was still in denial, in shock and had no tools to even attempt to heal.

I've heard of some losing a teenage child, some at six weeks in the womb, and others stillborn at full-term. Every child and every experience is different and I can't compare what I went through to my friend's stillbirth experience but it felt like the Band-Aid on the hole in my soul was traumatically ripped off. I bawled. I had to leave work. I cried all the way thru the mountains and back to my apartment where I curled in a ball and sobbed for hours.

2009

In early 2009, I graduated with a doctorate degree in chiropractic and experienced many great things, yet it wasn't until I met my future husband one random night that I started to be able to verbalize my smashed and broken heart without hyperventilating or tears, or both. Meeting him was like a breath of fresh ocean air and was he hot!

I was out on the town with my friends. We were sitting outside at a table in beautiful sunny California when randomly someone asked to buy me a drink. I had gone out that night with the main purpose being to consume beverages, so I said yes.

I'm a fan of easy conversation and the way ours was going felt like I had known him for YEARS. He was charming, gentlemanly, witty, respectful, and fearless! Given my prior year, I had great difficulty in relating to that fearless feeling, like I had prior to the pregnancy. It was like it slipped away from me. It was so attractive so see in him that it became contagious.

I felt calm and comfortable the more we got to know each other. His questions were real and the conversations had substance. He wanted to learn as much as possible about me and he cared about my opinions, which are usually strong. I had only known him a few days, yet his fearlessness was extremely inspiring. It was then, for the first time, that I was able to share that piece of my story with a stranger so courageously. I didn't hyperventilate, I didn't even pause, and no tears.

From that point on, it got easier and easier to say it out loud. The waves of downs and ups would still come randomly. The nine months I lived in California were filled with fun, with productive learning for my future career and most loudly filled with learning about myself. My knowledge of how to attract the ideal client, how to market, how to advertise, how to network, and most importantly how to be ME, were all increasing by the hour.

I was impatiently waiting on my scores from the part four board exam to be able to fully wear the hat of Chiropractor when I decided to go to Las Vegas for a birthday party. While hungover the morning after the birthday party, I got word that a chiropractor was retiring in my hometown and the timing was perfect for my career. After some deliberation in my own head, my soul felt comfortable in the decision to move back home to Nebraska. Luckily for me, that hot man I had just met decided to come with me.

So, after only three months of knowing each other, we took the plunge and moved halfway across the country, from California to Nebraska. Had my experience with the twins not happened, my career today, my appreciation for life, my ability to speak life into others and my deep love for my family would not be possible, at least not in the way I know it. For me, to know loss is to then appreciate what I am given. To know death is to then appreciate life. To know sadness is to then appreciate joy.

Waves

I know for a fact that God is real. Not that a doubt ever existed in my head, but it is now very obvious that God has to be real. Even before motherhood, just studying the human anatomy system in its complexity proved to me the existence of God. I also know that He works in ways we may not understand - ever! I can't quite say that I can fully wrap my brain around the experience of the twins but I know their existence was meant to change my life and it sure did.

After I moved back to Nebraska I started to see patients. It was in my second week in practice and my new patient that morning was only two weeks old. The minute I read her age on the chart I was hit with a frozen feeling. I hadn't held a baby since I had held my twins. How had I not thought about having tiny babies as patients and having to hold them? I was so nervous. I was fearful. I didn't know what I was feeling completely.

The moment came that I had to get up to go in the room. I was the doctor, that baby was my patient. I took a slow deep breath and opened the door. I walked in and this sweet little thing looked right up at me and I smiled. I felt an instant connection. I chatted with the mother for a few minutes before evaluating the baby. This poor thing hadn't pooped in ten days! Poor thing. Poop that hangs out is like poison. Get it out and get it out daily - just saying. The baby had just been to the medical doctor who gave them a prescription to help with the constipation. I was their stop on the way to the pharmacy.

I assessed her spine delicately and was confident that I isolated the problem areas. I applied gentle minimal pressure and the bones shifted back into alignment easily. I then talked about the brain-body connection with the mother, rescheduled them for a follow-up and sent them on their way.

I learned later that this little one had a giant blow out diaper no more than ten minutes after my adjustment while waiting in line for her prescription! Whoooohoooooooo! That was success. I felt warm fuzzy butterflies of accomplishment. It was an overwhelming feeling of being in the right place at the right time. That, in my opinion, is how God speaks. Serendipitously. That was one patient encounter of many that affirmed the connection we as humans have with others – that we cannot give without also simultaneously receiving.

A few days later, after feeling so great about changing the life of that little one, I was hit with a tsunami of a different kind of wave. My cousin was expecting and had stopped in the office to show me her ultrasound pictures. Again, a year after the twins, I was overwhelmed with instant hyperventilation. I tried my best to hold back my tears, but this was the first ultrasound picture I had seen since. The trigger was so strong. I was happy for her, I truly was. I had extreme difficulty expressing that happiness given my internal stir.

I felt like all I did was work, so regular triggers didn't seem to bother so much anymore. I could now look at a double stroller without wanting to literally punch someone. Progress! However, after seeing those ultrasound pictures, I went home and cried for hours.

To anyone who has ever lost a child, it sucks, plain and simple. It's often overwhelming when you actually think about the inability for you to simply hug them ever again. I agree that it is better to know love and lose it, then never to know love at all, but the struggle to want to hold something unavailable is as real as actually holding them.

2011

Throughout life there are many, MANY choices you can make. Growing up, decisions held less weight in the responsibility category than those that now involve my family, especially my children. Sometimes I wonder if I get too heated about my beliefs, opinions and choices since I missed the opportunity to do so with my twins. Nevertheless, I like what I like, I know what I know and I choose what resonates with my soul and my intuition.

Some friends of mine have chosen to have their baby at home, most of those in water. It has been recently sternly voiced to me by a health professional at a local hospital that some see this choice as unsafe, unhealthy, and possibly negligent.

In general, denying someone the right to choose that which clearly is given and legal is becoming more and more popular by the day. Seriously! Without choice, we are not humans - you know that free will thing? Yeah, THAT.

Due to the possibility of needing immediate help given my experience with the twins, I felt more comfortable having a hospital to birth for my next child. I became pregnant in 2011, and given my previous experience, I was filled me with fear on a daily basis.

Fear is an absolute liar. Fear never accomplished anything, and even knowing this, it was impossible for me to shake! Negative, unproductive thoughts commonly repeated in my mind. Will this baby be ok? Will I go into preterm labor? Will I get to take her home? Will I get to hear her voice?

Sleep seemed to help, so I slept a lot; about ten hours a night. Talking about the fear with friends and family helped somewhat, but it was very difficult to shake completely. I was never given a reason why the twins came too soon, so it's almost as if I expected something bad to happen. Tell me how a woman can be expected to stay positive about having a successful pregnancy and the ability to bring the baby home, after such an unsuccessful one!

I remember having the conversation with my husband about vaccination when I was pregnant. All I had to do to get the window of confusion opened in his brain, is show him the current schedule compared to when I was born in 1982. Back then there were less than 15 on the schedule, TOTAL. Now in 2016, that number has more than tripled. [1] He immediately wanted to know more. It was an easy, awesome conversation. He agreed that our choice to say no thank you was the best choice.

My labor started three days (not three months - thank you Jesus), before the anticipated due date. Then came the choices. I learned later that some mothers in this country do not even know that these choices exist!

Little miss independent came out with the cord around her neck, she was blue and she was taken elsewhere for an hour. My husband and my mother quickly volunteered to go with her while my fabulous doctor patched me up. So we did not have the choice to harvest the cord blood or to delay cord clamping. Also, I was unable to delay her bath, which would have allowed the natural substances to soak into her skin. Thankfully, after that hour, she came back into the room as healthy as I could imagine and I could then hold her for the first time.

I accepted the Vitamin K shot – It was like I was wearing stilettos while walking on a fence with this one, but I said yes. There are mixed reviews from the research I was given, so again I followed my intuition.

For Kinley, I also accepted the antibiotic eye drops. She is and has always been super healthy. The pharmacy learned her name at age three, for what? Antibiotic eye drops. What an ironic coincidence.

I politely declined all vaccines with the presence of a bacteria or a virus in them, which is all except the vitamin K, for my daughter and for myself. In the hospital, while fatigued and hormonal, the nurse was super persistent that I had made the wrong choice. That's the thing about hormones just one day after having a baby. They dissolve my filter of proper or professional communication. With both this nurse and later the pediatrician, I had to quickly know my stuff and stand up for my choices. Both conversations ended in my wish for them to stop asking questions. That's another thing about freedom of choice. If I have a right to say no, why can't it just be left at that? Why is a lengthy conversation about risks needed when my NO should just be enough?

Even the choice of which bubble bath to use was important to me. I settled on a product with a recognizable ingredient list. When comparing a simple list to that of more popular, cheaper companies, I was surprised by how many foreign unnatural ingredients were present.

I used the rule of recognizing ingredients also when choosing nutrition options, since I breastfed. What I ate became what she ate so I chose wisely to get her the needed ingredients. I know some people have difficulty breastfeeding, but if it's at all possible, DO IT! It's one of the most important choices you can make to positively affect the health of your child.

That's the thing I love about my choices, they are MINE and MINE alone to make. If you don't agree, cool - just get the hell out of my way. When having a baby, some things you think will be a choice and end up being unavailable. A birth plan is good, even though they are usually difficult to follow entirely. I like to think that this is God's way of telling us we are not in control.

2015

When I became pregnant again in 2015, fear still was determined to be my friend. Having a healthy and thriving three-year-old at home calmed that fear a GOOD notch, but not completely. Each day seemed to get better and I wasn't sleeping excessive amounts.

At thirty-seven weeks pregnant, I learned from my doctor that she was breech. As a Chiropractor, I knew there were some possible techniques for the sole purpose of making the ligaments and pelvic alignment completely symmetrical to then allow gravity to pull the baby's head down. I visited my team of chiropractors and nothing worked!

I was forced to schedule a C-Section with my doctor for the Wednesday before her due date, only a few days early. I now had to mentally prepare for more choices. An epidural was inevitable given the C-Section.

I again accepted the Vitamin K shot, and this time I declined the antibiotic eye drops. I remembered recently visiting a friend in the hospital who just had a baby. I witnessed the application of the drops and the look on his face. The acceptance of them no longer settled well with my gut.

I also continued in my pattern to decline all vaccines that contained bacteria or viruses - which was all vaccines except the Vitamin K shot. The difference this time in the reaction to my choice was that I gave the health professionals ample warning that I was to decline them.

Each mother planning to give birth at my local hospital was and is required to attend a meeting while still pregnant to get paperwork and such in order. I vividly remember filling out many papers. I had a few extra papers in my stack since I knew ahead of time of my choices.

All the other mothers looked over at me extremely confused as to why I had more forms. None of the other mothers - or fathers for that matter - even knew that some of these choices existed. We should all have the right to choose and be given the option of that choice.

I wrote in giant letters on the forms - "No Vaccines. Tell Nurses to not ask. Thanks!" No one asked. It was lovely. My two daughters now, in 2016, are extremely healthy and they fill my heart with an everlasting unconditional love and joy that is beyond words.

The meaning of life for me, with only my short thirty-three years on this planet, is LOVE. I also have an aching need to leave a significant impact in the world. That want fuels me on a daily basis. Being a mother, being a doctor and having opinions fulfills that need for me.

They say that you know you are an activist when you are unable to control a deep feeling - not just a thought - about a particular subject. I'll always remember the first moment of my first experience with this heart-pounding deep-feeling. I must get slightly political to insure clear understanding of the sequence of events that led up to this moment.

California - where I used to reside - had just passed SB277 - to mandate vaccines in all public schools. Instantly I had a new found appreciation for Nebraska's religious exemption to vaccinations. A right that I still had, NO LONGER existed there. Sad. I told my heartbroken friends who still lived there to just send their kids to private or home school, which takes a good amount of pennies. Although some options still existed if they chose not to vaccinate, the right to choose was being admonished and THAT pissed me right off.

So, I was still slightly hormonal from recent motherhood - my husband would add more than slightly - so my fuse of possible pissed off level was maybe a little short. I continued to read, to listen and I tried my best not to react, but then I got pissed again.

That "stand up against abortion" thing I learned in high school from a priest in theology class continued to speak to me. I'd known about the aborted fetal material in vaccines from that priest in high school, but it really only pissed me off when the right to say no thank you and still attend school got taken away.

Why? Well first of all there is ABORTED FETAL MATERIAL in vaccines. I wished that pissed off more people, especially those who took the same classes in school, but it seemed to only concern some. Many people were surprised.

Soon after SB277 was passed, I received an email from my state Chiropractic association, containing a document titled: *APPENDIX TO IMMUNIZATION POLICY FOR THE ARCHDIOCESE OF OMAHA*[2]. The third paragraph on the first page states: "Currently, vaccines for Rubella and Chicken Pox are derived from cell lines originated from aborted fetuses and there are no alternatives available in the United States. Submitting to these vaccines constitutes passive and remote material cooperation in EVIL." [2]

Now that was only TWO SENTENCES from the extremely wordy document, but that's all I needed to confirm my feeling. Evil. Black and white. Plain and simple. Gross. The rest of the document then tries to justify why we should still agree to injecting these evil substances into ourselves and our children.

Look - Jesus help us - If you go to the CDC's (Centers for Disease Control and Prevention) website (www.cdc.gov/vaccines) [1] all info is listed. A diploid lung fibroblast from aborted fetal tissue was the cell line used to derive the MMR vaccine, that is still used today [1]. Other vaccines currently on the schedule also contain aborted fetal material. These ingredients are not simply called ABORTED BABIES. Instead, they are coded as: MRC-5, WI-38, RA273, PER C6 and HEK 293 [1].

A living cell, whether from an aborted fetus or from a chicken or cow, allows a genetic code of that species to be an ingredient in the vaccine to then purposefully interact with our existing genetic code to then create an ARTIFICIAL (not natural) immune response. This genetic code works as the glue or the hook to allow the vaccine to have the intended cause and effect inside our body.

Although frustrated for others, given that Nebraska still allowed a religious exemption to vaccinations I kept my mouth shut.... until.... July 2015. In July, Planned Parenthood was soon to be investigated for selling parts of aborted babies. I started to voice my opinions publically via social media and I seemed to be more pissed than others. I received many messages and comments in support of my opinion. I was able to allow the positive response from those around me to enlighten my soul.

I learned soon after of a U.S. Senator from Nebraska who co-authored a bill to defund Planned Parenthood. It was a start! I then found out that same U.S. Senator was having a community conversation in my hometown. I went with the intention of listening. A sweet old lady quickly changed the subject from the Iran Deal, (that's a whole other book) to the Planned Parenthood scandal. Immediately my heart jumped out of my chest. It was comparable to volleyball two-a-day practices in high school with only being seated. Boom. Boom. Like a fire was being lit for me to stand up and shout. Activist. I was officially one in that moment.

After she said her point, I raised my hand. Fearlessly, I jumped up and it went something like this:

Hi, I'm Dr. Kim, a Chiropractor here in town. Senator I think what you are doing is awesome, yet I struggle to see optimism to defund Planned Parenthood. What they appeared to be doing in those videos made me want to literally vomit on the floor. Aborted fetuses are used for medical research, funded by Big Pharma who has an astronomical income, larger than all incomes in this community combined, so I have difficulty understanding how you can so optimistic.

From that point on, I received so many responses, it was incredible. Even at the store in my small town, people I had never met stopped to tell me how glad they were that I said what I said. I quickly realized that MANY others in my community felt similarly about abortion and my Facebook friends list seemed to instantly rise to the MAX of five thousand. I took that as a job well done. I'm still an activist in my personal life, whenever an opportunity presents itself.

By merely speaking my opinion out loud, it felt like I conquered fear and won. Freedom of choice in this country is very interesting to me. I wish we all fought harder to keep this right.

2016

Now, in 2016, I am a wife and a mother, of two beautiful little girls. The love I feel for them is so tender and sweet to my soul. I know that without having the experience of the twins, I wouldn't be as able to see these beautiful girls as the two angels they are. They are gifts.

I surely know that life is short and today is the only day I live in. At my office, I treat each patient as a new refreshing opportunity to give and to also gain something - a piece to fill up my soul you could say. I gain great fulfillment in helping others.

I am blessed with the opportunity to now help bunches of people in my office. I have strong confidence, not just as a Doctor, but also as a person. I would not know complete calm, confident comfortability without having experienced complete fear and loss. I may forever feel like a puzzle piece is missing in my heart. The exact shape to fit the hole only exists in Heaven. I can only hope and use the tools I've learned to help the triggers and waves hit me less often.

Life is bittersweet and now-a-days mostly sweet. My world had been spun around and from it I gained a deep appreciation for living, which then lead to the ability to be comfortable in my

own body again. I strive daily to change the world for the better, whether it be in my interactions with my family, my interactions with my patients or my interactions with those that have the power to make laws.

Recently, I felt comfortable enough in my own skin to speak to local senators and the Governor of my state to ask their opinion of health. The current Governor of Nebraska, Pete Ricketts, explained why the mandated Meningitis bill was shot down so quickly here in Nebraska. He stated that the bill simply stated that more people DIE from the inoculation than from the disease itself. That was enough information for the senators and himself to vote no, and vote it quickly. We never know what tomorrow will bring, especially in the world of politics.

I do know that every one of us should be OUTRAGED about the ever increasing stripping of our FREEDOMS. One may say that my dislike for abortion is not in favor of freedom. I am not going to tell anyone what to do, just as I would wish for others to not tell me what to do. However, I do hope that the acknowledgement of a heartbeat in the early days of conception that indeed qualifies that fetus as a living being, could potentially teach women not to choose abortion.

I've now been in practice for almost seven years in Nebraska. It's so fun. I'm convinced that mostly its due to the fact that I am head over heels in love unconditionally with my family, my career and most importantly myself.

How I see myself in the mirror now, compared to my reaction in 2008 is totally different. You attract those who are attracted to you. What can I say? I'm an independent woman with opinions.

Most of the time, given today's society and popular thought as a whole, my opinions pave an awesomely unique trail, mainly against popular belief. Not even close to half of the population uses chiropractic care. That makes it unpopular as a whole. I devoted my career to striving daily to perfect the art of the natural healing chiropractic adjustment.

Natural Immunity

I received regular chiropractic adjustments as a baby and throughout life. I believe natural things intended to boost immunity should be introduced prior to unnatural things. This idea seems to also be unpopular in today's society, especially with the push of BIG PHARMA. Now don't get me wrong - medicine has its place and I'm not a medical doctor, but you better be sure of two things. First, I want a complete list of side effects before I put a lab-concocted substance into my body - or my child's for that matter. And second - your body was designed by the Creator to be self-healing. When you break a bone or scrape your knee, in time the body heals.

It seems to be less and less popular, at least in this country, to let the body's immune system fight and have established mechanisms through a daily lifestyle for a killer-strong immune system. Here are some of my opinions on how to build a healthy immune system:

-Your BODY TEMPERATURE should be around 98.6 degrees Fahrenheit to maintain homeostasis. When the body has a fever experience, it is reacting to a foreign situation. The body heats up to kill the foreign invader. Too hot of a fever is potentially harmful, yet in general fevers are a good thing. Staying warm, not too hot and not too cold, keeps your body at optimal temperatures for homeostasis to help keep you healthy.

-Your body heals when you REST and SLEEP. Our systems are able to slow down and some completely shut down during intensely restful periods. Hectic periods of adrenaline cause our body to stress which then typically makes it more difficult to heal.

-Exercise is essential to keep your vital body systems working properly. Exercise affects our physical structures, our hormones and therefore our moods.

-That old saying 'you are what you eat' is very impactful to me. Our bodies are constantly in a state of change. Cells in our body become completely different cells in time. Our bodies use what we feed it as fuel for the changes. Feed it well.

- Staying hydrated can also affect health significantly. As humans, our cells are comprised of water. Lots and lots of water. When fluids are absorbed by the body, we are able to better function which then positively affects health and mood. Drinking fluids with a slightly alkaline pH are better absorbed by our systems.

- Your brain communicates with your body through your nervous system, housed in your spine. Chiropractic adjustments allow the body to heal by removing nervous system interference. Regular chiropractic care is essential to maintaining health. I chose Chiropractic above all other health professions for my career, easily. I am in love with Chiropractic and its benefits and you should be too!

PERSPECTIVE

A successful career is only possible with the support of a successful family. A new friend of mine once told me to have a great practice, you must also have a great life. He was absolutely exact. Given my story of 2008, the missing puzzle piece in my heart is minutely fulfilled with each instance of love - whether it be towards my family or towards my patients. Helping others calms my soul.

If you have ever lost a child before, the most helpful words I could give is that the pain may never go away, but life will present you with opportunities to change your perspective, if you are willing and open to it. Time seems to heal a little, at least for me, but I don't ever expect the longing to hold the twins to go away completely.

Perhaps that is what helps stir up my want for all children to be healthy. Had I been given the opportunity to raise the twins in this life I would have chosen natural ways to keep them healthy. The biggest hiccup in society today for those choosing natural health is that it is an unpopular choice. Some don't even know in certain situations that options exist to choose other things, or to say no thank you completely.

My wish is for all to be able to have a right to choose that which they think is best for them and for their family and for that choice to be pressure-free. Pressures exist due to popular belief and the specific opinion of the healthcare provider you choose.

Telling the world that I chose not to vaccinate my children was almost slightly comparable to someone coming out of the closet. It is against what society sees as popular. Regardless of popular belief, I am one person, with my own belief system, and for myself and my family that is what I choose. As a United States citizen, in the land of the free and the home of the brave, I can only hope that others who no longer have an exemption to vaccination, simply for school attendance, will someday be given back that right.

Also, I can't stop contemplating the full meaning of informed consent. I recently attended Kindergarten round-up for my oldest daughter. Ninety percent of the time was spent talking about vaccinations. No words were offered to inform of the ingredients, the risks, or the option to say no thank you. My husband kept nudging me and I did my best to bite my tongue. I stayed silent and calmly gave my religious exemption form to the secretary after the meeting.

Various people have sent me messages asking for advice on how to proceed when they try to enter a professional school where vaccines are required. Many people are unaware that a titer test may be an option, to prove that you have the immune response already present in your system to a certain disease. When you encounter a disease, either naturally or artificially, your body then creates a response. That response can lead to the productions of antibodies, the fighters that help kill that specific disease if you were to encounter it again. I ABSOLUTELY LOVE when someone receives a titer test for something they have NOT been vaccinated for and it shows that antibodies are present. We encounter disease frequently by simply living life and breathing the air. We often win the fight against disease without even knowing it, given that antibodies may form without any symptom of disease.

That's the thing about informed consent. Informed implies that the person receiving such procedures has an adequate, clear understanding of the facts (ingredients) and consequences (risks/side effects) of such procedure. I often hear that the ingredients and side effects of vaccines are not offered. If all were given the option to say no thank you, to have a choice, most likely more people would then say no, feeling more comfortable with that choice.

If that were the only hiccup – I mean after a mother says no thank you, it's rarely that simple. In my case, when I was in the hospital for the birth of my first child, the nurse came in to ask me again if I wanted vaccines for myself and my child. She used fear tactics about "people dying in California" to try to get me to change my mind. If I really had a freedom of choice, why wasn't it respected? Why couldn't it be that simple? Why couldn't my NO THANK YOU the FIRST time be enough to not be asked again? It was obviously not the answer she wanted. That was quite apparent. However, I wished and still wish that my choice was more respected, the first time I made it.

That wish was my inspiration for writing this book. I have a strong hope that mothers all over the world will one day be able to say no thank you to forced medical procedures without pressure, without question and without negativity from those offering the procedure. I have received multiple messages from mothers scared to say no at the medical doctor. They ask me for recommendations for a provider that won't make them feel bad for choosing to say no thank you.

In high school, we talked about peer pressure being something that was super influential and how to watch out for it. Well, I find myself still watching out for it, not only for me and my family, but also for others. If no thank you was simply a good enough answer, since we should have a freedom of choice, pressure to then change our mind would not be offered.

Guilt and fear are easily thrown in when your choice disagrees with those offering the procedure. I hear often of mothers forced to find a new pediatrician for merely declining vaccines for their child. Pediatricians are allowed to do so, however my blood pressure instantly rises. Uh, freedom of choice, anyone?

Russia, France and other countries have already declared that they will not mandate vaccinations – for the ENTIRE country. Awesome. Here in the United States, that is not the case. The current government has left it up to the states to decide for themselves. Why? Well, I can only speculate.

Now don't get me wrong. Vaccines exist. However, forcing ANY medical procedure is where I have the issue. Had I grown up being fully vaccinated, perhaps I may feel differently...but I wasn't. Neither were my siblings. Neither were my children. That is a choice for the parents to make. Children should belong to the parents, not the government.

I now strive daily to make a wave in the world regarding the issues of abortion and vaccination. When politicians are around me, I speak up – loudly and quickly. It is my simple hope that freedom of choice and informed consent will have true meaning in the medical world soon, especially in the United States.

To the parents of the world, especially those who have lost a child before, hold your children tight. They are gifts. It is YOUR responsibility to take care of them as you see fit. It's your choice. Choose wisely and without fear. Life is too short to fear anything, for tomorrow is never guaranteed. I will continue to fight for freedom of choice and for healthy options, to do my part to make the world a healthier place for my children and for all children.

REFERENCES

1. http://www.cdc.gov/vaccines

2. Appendix to Immunization Policy for the Archdiocese of Omaha.

www.ingramcontent.com/pod-product-compliance
Lightning Source LLC
Chambersburg PA
CBHW060409190526
45169CB00002B/818